*"Who can recognize
his own mistakes?
..... for mistakes
(he is) unaware of."
(Psalm 19:12).*

*"Your word is a lamp
to guide me and
a light for my path."
(Psalm 119:105).*

Copyright © 2019 by Afterlife Matters.

All rights reserved. No part of this publication may be used or reproduced, stored in a retrieval system or transmitted in any form or by any means, electronic, mechanical, photocopying, recording, scanning, or otherwise, except as permitted under Section 107 or 108 of the 1976 United States Copyright Act, without written permission.

CHRISTIANITY: FAITH OR MYTH
Afterlife Matters

ISBN: 978-0-578-52513-6

Library of Congress Control Number: 2019906992

Printed in the USA, UK, and Australia

TABLE OF CONTENTS

Chapter 1: Christianity in America 7

Chapter 2: Not Evangelism
But Discipleship 15

Chapter 3: Exodus and Salvation 21

Chapter 4: Christian Faith and
the Devil's Faith 31

Chapter 5: Majority and Minority 37

Chapter 6: God is In the Detail 43

Chapter 7: Grace, Faith, and Reward 49

Chapter 8: Deny Yourself and Take Up
Your Cross 55

Chapter 9: You Must Not Have Any Other God
But Me 65

Chapter 10: First Love 73

Contemplation 79

"When you hear
His voice today,
don't be stubborn ....."
(Hebrews 3:15).

"I correct and discipline
everyone I love.
Take this seriously
and repent!"
(Revelations 3:19).

Dr. D. James Kennedy:

"The vast majority of people who are members of churches in America today are not Christians. I base it on the empirical evidence of 24 years of examining tens of thousands of those people on what they are basing their hopes of eternal life, and it's not Jesus Christ! It is merely their own morality, their own piety and their own goodness."

CHAPTER 1
CHRISTIANITY IN AMERICA

It is a fact that Christianity shares the largest slice of the belief pie in the world today:

Christianity (32.8%)
Islam (22.5%)
Hindu (13.8%)
Buddha (7.2%)
Judaism (0.2%)
Atheism / Agnosticism (11.8%)
Other (11.8%)

It is a fact that no country has more Christians than the United States, with nearly 240 million souls or almost 75% of its population.

However, a recent survey by LifeWay Research found that the majority of American Christians are, in fact, *"heretics"*!

Proof #1: In general, American Christians appear to agree that Jesus died on the cross for sin and that He rose from the dead.

Proof #2: Most of them, however, think that *"religious belief is a matter of personal opinion, not about objective truth"*.

Proof #3: 52% say that *"most people are basically good"*.

In fact, Romans 3:10 says, *"No one is righteous—not even one."*

Proof #4: 51% say that *"God accepts the worship of all religions, including those who believe in many gods"*.

In fact, John 14:6, *"I am the way, the truth, and the life. No one comes to the Father except through Me."*

Proof #5: 78% say that *"Jesus was the first and greatest being created by God the Father"*.

In fact, John 1:1 says, *"In the beginning was the Word, and the Word was with God, and the Word was God."*

So, which Bible that the majority of American Christians actually read?

Which God in whom they believe?

Which Christ in whom they have faith?

Or which one in whom they don't?

American Bible Society and Barna Group also found a fact that:

"32% of American Christians never read the Bible.
12% read it less than once a year.
8% read it once or twice a year.
8% read it three or four times a year.
6% read it once a month
8% read it once a week.
13 read it several times a week.
Only 14% read it every day."

The word is out that many of the nearly 75% of the country who call themselves "Christians" don't take their faith seriously!

A study in 1995-1996 may offer a hint:

"71% of Christians in the US converted before the age of 14."

CHAPTER 1 CHRISTIANITY IN AMERICA

Back in 1937, Jesse Overholtzer founded Child Evangelism Fellowship, an organization that focuses on evangelizing children between the ages of 4 and 14 years. The *"4-14 window"* is believed to be *"the most receptive and often the most effective agents for mission in evangelizing their peer group."*

A 2003 Barna research showed that children are *"the most population segment to minister due to their spiritual 'teachability' and developmental 'vulnerability'"*.

"The implication of these findings is clear," claims Barna. *"Anyone who wishes to have significant influence on the development of a person's moral and spiritual foundations had better exert that influence while the person is still open-minded and impressionable— in other words, while the person is still young."*

Bryant Myers and Dan Brewster also argue that *"global evangelism programs should target younger children for conversion because the clay is still soft and children need our attention more urgently than any other group of people"*.

However, scientists point that children's *"teachability and vulnerability"* may be attributed to their brain development condition.

Humans' brains are in fact still developing, even until ages 11-14, their brains are not steady enough for high level reasoning and decision making.

Introducing salvation to the premature without teaching its significance in Christian faith is nothing short of oversimplifying.

Teaching the uncritical to accept a genuine depiction of salvation has proven to be indoctrination and *"mythification"* (= causing to become a myth).

While it is obvious that 4-14 window proves to be the golden window for evangelism and every other ism, it also poses the greatest risks of superficial conversions and false understanding of the faith.

Not to mention manipulating children into confessing faith in ideas they're clueless about.

Not surprisingly, it was found that vast majority of those making decisions for Christ at a young age were falling away from the faith.

Rev. Ray Comfort revealed that in 1991, the first year of the *"Decade of Harvest"*, a major denomination with 11,500 churches in the US managed to harvest 294,000 decisions for Christ.

At the end of the day, the churches could only find 14,000 in fellowship and simply couldn't account for 280,000 of their decisions.

Data from the Southern Baptist Convention in 2001 indicates that they are currently losing 70%-88% of their youth after their freshman year in college.

70% of teenagers who are involved in church youth groups stop attending church within two years of their high school graduation.

Report from Southern Baptist Council on Family Life in 2002 reveals that 88% of the children in evangelical homes leave church at 18.

Tom Bisset interviewed Christian kids and asked them when, why, and how they abandoned their faith:

Finding #1. They left because they had troubling, unanswered questions about the faith

Finding #2. They left because their faith was not *"working"* for them

Finding #3. They left because they allowed other things to take priority

Finding #4. They left because they never personally owned their faith

Precisely as described in Matthew 13:5-7:

"Some fell on rocky ground, where it did not have much soil. It sprang up quickly, because the soil was shallow. But when the sun rose, the seedlings were scorched, and they withered because they had no root.

Other seed fell among thorns, which grew up and choked the seedlings."

CHAPTER 2
NOT EVANGELISM
BUT DISCIPLESHIP

It is a fact that evangelism is most effective among kids.

But, is evangelizing the young biblical?

What do the Scriptures say about the evangelization of children?

"You have been taught the holy Scriptures from childhood, and they have given you the wisdom to receive the salvation that comes by trusting in Christ Jesus." (2 Timothy 3:15)

"I remember your genuine faith, for you share the faith that first filled your grandmother Lois and your mother, Eunice. And I know that same faith continues strong in you." (2 Timothy 1:5).

Yes, it is a fact that teaching God's Word to children is in line with the Scriptures.

However, the Scriptures also warn:

"And whoever welcomes a child like this in My name welcomes Me. These little ones believe in Me. It would be best for the person

who causes one of them to lose faith to be drowned in the sea with a large stone hung around his neck." (Matthew 18:5-6).

"As long as you live, you, your children, and your grandchildren must fear the LORD your God. All of you must obey all his laws and commands that I'm giving you, and you will live a long time." (Deuteronomy 6:2).

"Parents, don't be hard on your children. Raise them properly. Teach them and instruct them about the Lord." (Ephesians 6:4).

"Be careful about the way you live and about what you teach. Keep on doing this, and you will save not only yourself, but the people who hear you." (1 Timothy 4:16).

"They must be silenced, because they are turning whole families away from the truth by their false teaching. And they do it only for money." (Titus 1:11).

"Parents, don't be hard on your children. If you are, they might give up." (Colossians 3:21).

"I encourage you to follow my example."
(1 Corinthians 4:16).

*"I never stop thanking God for you.
I always remember you in my prayers."*
(Ephesians 1:16).

*"Go to the people of all nations and make them
my disciples. Baptize them in the name of the
Father, the Son, and the Holy Spirit, and teach
them to do everything I have told you.
I will be with you always, even until the end of
the world."* (Matthew 28:19-20).

Yes, you should evangelize children,
but do not neglect other important things:

#1. Watch your doctrine
#2. Be their role models
#3. Pray for them continuously

As a matter of fact, the Great Commission is
not evangelism but discipleship.

Discipleship is a spiritual adoption. It is not just
one time conversion but life transformation.

CHAPTER 2 NOT EVANGELISM BUT DISCIPLESHIP

It is not developing a foundation for them but building a house on solid rock with them!

"Anyone who hears and obeys these words of mine is like a wise person who built a house on solid rock. Rain poured down, rivers flooded, and winds beat against that house. But it was built on solid rock, and so it did not fall." (Matthew 7:24-25).

Otherwise, when *"the rain falls, the flood comes, and the winds beat against that house, and it collapses; it is utterly destroyed!"* (Matthew 7:27).

There are many people out there who were born and raised in Christian households, went to Christian schools, even served the Lord in church choirs and whatnots—only to have started to question, to doubt their faith in the process, and to denounce their faith in Christ down the stretch.

Arthur Schopenhauer argued that due to capacity for believing is strongest in childhood, teaching some doctrines of belief to this tender age could foster more resistance to doubting those doctrines later on.

In fact, a 2018 Pew Research Center Report proved that young Christians are leaving the church these days:

They question a lot of religious teaching, they don't like religious organizations, they don't like religious leaders, they think religion is irrelevant to them, they no longer believe it's true, and etc etc.

As the Scripture says, *"Great was the fall of it!"*

There are no shortcuts to discipleship.

It doesn't take long to fall in love with Christ but it does take a lifelong to stay in love with Him.

It doesn't take time to convert but it does take a lifetime to be like Christ.

Do not make children Christian converts!

They are not statistics.

CHAPTER 3
EXODUS AND SALVATION

The Exodus of the Old Testament is a historical event that begins from the Israelites' freedom from slavery in Egypt to the promised land.

Salvation of the New Testament is a historical event that begins from the freedom out of the slave market of sin to the kingdom of God.

Exodus is the Israelite journey and salvation is the Christian journey.

After Israel's exodus, salvation was prepared for the world to free it from greater slavery.

The Exodus timeline consists of three stages:

Stage I. Redemption
Stage II. Righteousness
Stage III. Worship

After God delivered the Israelites from slavery in Egypt, He simply did not "teleport" them to the promised land!
As a matter of fact, each of them had to go on foot in the wilderness to the destination.

Along the way, God gave them the moral law to follow, so that they would live in righteousness.

Because only the righteous can come to worship God!

"When you bring the people out of Egypt, all of you will worship God on this mountain." (Exodus 3:12b).

"Who may go up the LORD's mountain? Who may stand in His holy place? Only those who do right for the right reasons, and don't worship idols or tell lies under oath." (Psalms 24:3-4).

The stages of this sequence can't be violated.

You must be redeemed first in order to be righteous in God's sight.

Unless you are righteous, you can't worship God.

Each stage of the exodus applies to the stages of salvation's timeline:

"Jesus answered, 'I am the way, the truth, and the life. No one goes to the Father except through Me.'" (John 14:6).

Stage I. Way
Stage II. Truth
Stage III. Life

Atonement for the sins of the world was offered by Christ on Calvary.

Only those who believes in Him and accepts His atonement will be redeemed from the slave market of sin.

Without atonement, there could be no redemption.

Atonement is the only way to be redeemed from the slave market of sin.

That's the *"way"*, the path, or *"the wilderness"* to the destination.

"Moses and his law are the truth."
(A Jewish saying).

Along the way, Jesus gave the
redeemed His truth, His laws:

Law I:
*"Love the Lord your God with all your heart,
with all your soul, with all your mind,
and with all your strength."*

Law II:
"Love others as much as you love yourself."

*"No other commandment is
more important than these two."*
(Mark 12:31).

*"For it is not those who hear the law who are
righteous in God's sight, but it is those who
obey the law who will be declared righteous."*
(Romans 2:13).

Until you're redeemed, you can't be righteous.
Until you're righteous, you won't see life.

*"And they (the unrighteous) will go away into
eternal punishment, but the righteous will go
into eternal life."* (Matthew 25:46).

"But we wait for what God has promised: new heavens and a new earth, where righteousness will be at home." (2 Peter 3:13).

The exodus and salvation are *"pilgrimages"*!

Egypt → Wilderness → Canaan.

Old life → Christian Life → Kingdom of God.

Redemption → Righteousness → Worship.

In salvation, God, the Father, the Son, and the Spirit play Their own role:

#1. God, the Father provided His love and initiated salvation by giving His begotten Son to the world that is *"hellbound"*.

"For God so loved the world, that He gave His only begotten Son, ..." (John 3:16a).

#2. The Son came to the world to:

A. *"Offer"* atonement
B. *"Promise"* eternal life

Christ died for all. The atonement for sin on Calvary was universal, final, one and done.

However, only those who has faith in Him will be redeemed from the slave market of sin.

They are no longer on *"one-way ride"* to eternal death or *"deathbound"*, but are now on the way to eternal life or *"lifebound"*.

"We know that we have crossed over from death to life ....." (1 John 3:14).

They are no longer slaves to sin but God and in His righteousness.

"Now you are free from your slavery to sin and you have become slaves who do what God approves of." (Romans 6:18).

"But if you keep on being faithful right to the end, you will be saved." (Matthew 24:13).

"He will give everlasting life to those who search for glory, honor, and immortality by persisting in doing what is good." (Romans 2:7).

#3. The Holy Spirit was sent to continue where Jesus left off.

"Then I will ask the Father to send you the Holy Spirit who will help you and always be with you." (John 14:16).

"The Helper whom I will send to you from the Father will come. This Helper, the Spirit of Truth who comes from the Father, will declare the truth about Me." (John 15:26).

"The Spirit will come and convict the world of its sin, and of God's righteousness, and of the coming judgment." (John 16:8).

"The Spirit shows what is true and will come and guide you into the full truth. The Spirit doesn't speak on His own. He will tell you only what He has heard from Me, and He will let you know what is going to happen." (John 16:13).

"There could be no redemption without the atonement, but if redemption is not appropriated the atonement still remains.

The work of atonement was the act of one person, but redemption involves several agencies. Christ, by suffering the death of the cross, made the atonement.

In effecting redemption, the subject works, the teacher works in presenting God's truth, the Holy Spirit works and applies the Gospel with power to the heart.

By this threefold agency redemption is effected.

The atonement came without the world's request; but redemption never comes without the earnest seeking of the individual.

The atonement was an event that took place 'once for all' at one period, on Calvary, two thousand years ago.

Redemption is constantly taking place in all parts of the world, and in all periods of human history.

This is the correct Biblical distinction between the two theological terms as used in the Scriptures."
(R. Venting).

CHAPTER 4
CHRISTIAN FAITH AND THE DEVIL'S FAITH

While statistics indicate that 12% of the world population today are doubtful or do not believe in the existence of God, ironically, the Bible proves that 0% of the devils are either atheists or agnostics:

"You surely believe there is only one God. That's fine. Even demons believe this, and it makes them shake with fear."
(James 2:19)

Statistics show that 33% of the world population may have confessed that Jesus is Son of God, the Bible in fact proves that 100% of the devils do so:

"They shouted, 'Jesus, Son of God, what do you want with us? Have you come to punish us before our time?'" (Matthew 8:29).

"Jesus from Nazareth, what do you want with us? Have you come to destroy us? I know who you are! You are God's Holy One." (Mark 1:24).

CHAPTER 4 CHRISTIAN FAITH AND THE DEVIL'S FAITH

Some Christians may pray to God the Father. In fact, all of the devils continually do so:

"Jesus said, 'Simon, listen to Me. Satan has asked to sift you like wheat.'"
(Luke 22:31)

Some Christians may believe that Jesus is the only Savior. In fact, all of the devils do so:

"She used to follow Paul and shout, 'These men are servants of the Most High God. They're telling you how you can be saved.'"
(Acts 16:17).

On July 15, 1859, Charles Blondin or as known as *"The Daredevil of Niagara Falls"*, walked 160 feet above the falls a few times back and forth as a huge crowd watched with shock and awe.

He crossed in a sack, on a bicycle, then with a stove and cooked an omelet!

After pushing a wheelbarrow across while blindfolded, he stopped and asked the audience:

"Do you believe I can carry a person across in this wheelbarrow?"

The crowd shouted that they believe!

"Now I need a volunteer in this wheelbarrow!"

None of them ever stepped forward that day.

Their faith claim in Charles Blondin proved to be not less and not more than just a fraud!

The Scriptures say:

If you believe in Christ, you will love Him. (1 John 5:1).

If you love Him, you will keep His commandments. (John 14:15).

Faith is determined by love.
Love is proven by obedience. (1 Peter 1:8a).

*"Obey God's message!
Don't fool yourselves by just listening to it."*
(James 1:22).

"Anyone who hears My teachings and doesn't obey them is like a foolish person who built a house on sand." (Matthew 7:26).

"The everlasting God ordered that what the prophets wrote must be shown to the people of every nation to bring them to the obedience of faith (obedience that is associated with faith)." (Romans 16:26).

Faith and obedience also prove to be interchangeable in their essence!

"And who did God say would never enter His place of rest? Weren't they the ones that 'disobeyed' Him? We see that those people did not enter the place of rest because they did not have 'faith'." (Hebrew 3:18-19).

"Without 'faith', no one can please God. Whoever goes to God must believe that God exists and that he rewards those who 'seek' Him." (Hebrews 11:6).

Consequently, nobody can please God and receive anything from Him without obedience!

"My friends, what good is it for one of you to say that you have faith if your actions do not prove it? Can that faith save you?" (James 2:14).

Because *"faith, if it is not accompanied by obedience, has no life in it— so long as it stands alone and dead!"* (James 2:17).

"Not everyone who calls me their Lord will get into the kingdom of heaven. Only the ones who obey my Father in heaven will get in." (Matthew 7:21).

Dietrich Bonhoeffer:
"Only he who believes is obedient, and only he who is obedient believes."

Now, what does your Christian faith require that the devils can't do?

CHAPTER 5
MAJORITY AND MINORITY

CHRISTIANITY: FAI†H OR *myth!*

With more than two billion believers, Christianity is unarguably the world's majority faith system.

For now.

However, what do the Scriptures say about *"majority"* (many) and *"minority"* (few)?

"They had disobeyed God while Noah was building the boat, but God had been patient with them. Only eight people were saved from drowning in that terrible flood." (1 Peter 3:20).

"Yet, God delivered just Lot because he was a righteous man who was sick of the shameful immorality of the wicked people around him." (2 Peter 2:7).

"But God was not pleased with many of those people, so their dead bodies were scattered over the desert." (1 Corinthians 10:5).

"With these 300 men I will rescue you and give you victory over the Midianites. Send all the others (29,700) home." (Judges 7:7).

CHAPTER 5 MAJORITY AND MINORITY

"But 7,000 Israelites have refused to worship Baal or kiss him, and they will live." (1 Kings 19:18).

"And Isaiah exclaims about Israel: 'Even if the people of Israel are as many as the grains of sand by the sea, yet only a few of them will be saved.'" (Romans 9:27).

"It is the same way now. God treated the people of Israel with undeserved grace, and so a few of them are still His followers." (Romans 11:5).

"I heard how many were sealed: 144,000. Those who were sealed were from every tribe of the people of Israel:" (Revelation 7:4).

"Because of what Jesus said, many of His disciples turned their backs on Him and stopped following Him." (John 6:66).

"Lord, are only a few people going to be saved?" Jesus answered: 'Do all you can to go in by the narrow door! A lot of people will try to get in, but will not be able to.'" (Luke 13:23-24).

"Go in through the narrow gate. The gate to destruction is wide, and the road that leads there is easy to follow. A lot of people go through that gate. But the gate to life is very narrow. The road that leads there is so hard to follow that only a few people find it."
(Matthew 7:13-14).

"On the judgment day many will call Me their Lord. They will say, 'We preached in Your name, and in Your name, we forced out demons and worked many miracles.' But I will tell them, 'I never knew you. Get away from Me, you who break God's laws.'" (Matthew 7:22-23).

"Therefore, many are invited, but few of those are chosen to stay." (Matthew 22:14).

"You will all die right here in the desert! Because you complained against Me, every one of you who is twenty years old or older and was included in the registration will die. You will not enter and occupy the land I swore to give you.
Only Caleb and Joshua will go in."
(Numbers 14:29-30).

CHAPTER 5 MAJORITY AND MINORITY

The paradigm of majority and minority in the Scriptures is loud and clear. It is, in fact, a plain and simple prophecy:

Many are called to be Christians, but few will receive eternal life.

Many are called to be Christian teachers and preachers, but few will enter the Kingdom of God.

Many of them, if not all, claim that they know Jesus, but in fact, Jesus never "knew" them!

To know Jesus is important. However, to be "known" by Jesus is more important.

In order to be "known" by Jesus, you must keep listening and following Him until you die!

"My sheep listen to My voice, I 'know' them, and they follow Me." (John 10:27).

Many proclaim their faith, but few put into practice.

Dr. James Binney:

"When I first became a Christian, I assumed that all church going people were automatically qualified for the fast track into heaven. It was a given. After becoming a church member, then a pastor, I had to rethink the issue.

I have encountered many leaders who doubted their faith, others who could not clearly explain how they were saved, and even others who frankly admitted that they had never been saved.

Imagine 20 pastors confessing their lost condition in one city!

It happened ..... when George Whitefield preached in Boston.

Dr. Bob Jones, Sr. said, 'I have spent nearly my entire life in association with ministers.

Nobody would tell you that every preacher in America is a saved man.'"

CHAPTER 6
GOD IS IN THE DETAIL

"For God so loved the world, that He gave His only begotten Son, that whosoever believeth in Him should not perish, but have everlasting life." (John 3:16).

"Write a Letter, Win a House: 'Homeowner selling $1.7M mansion for $25 and 'compelling' essay'." (An ad on social media).

Let's compare these two:

#1. Those two above are announcement headlines
#2. Those two are offers to the public
#3. They offer irresistible prizes
#4. The prizes, an *"everlasting life"* and a *"$1.7M mansion"*, are up for grabs

Like giveaways and promotions in general, offers also have their own details or as known as terms and conditions.

Terms and conditions are normally attached to a prize and mostly are non-negotiable.

CHAPTER 6 GOD IS IN THE DETAIL

Anyone who accepts the offer consequently declares to enter into a formal and legally binding contract with its terms and conditions.

Some of the Writing Contest's terms and conditions posted on the social media read:

"Paying $25 entry fee, writing 1-page story with 350 words maximum, one entry each person or household."

Any unmet terms and conditions will disqualify the participant.

As a *"headline"* offering salvation from God, where can you find John 3:16's *"see store for details"*, such as references, terms and conditions, or fine print in the Scripture?

One of them is on the following 20 verses:

"Whoever believes in the Son has everlasting life, but whoever disobeys the Son will not see life. Instead, the wrath of God remains on him." (John 3:36).

So, the word *"believe"* in John 3:16 is clearly not referring to Charles Blondin's "believers".

In fact, John 3:16 is all about nothing but the *"action"* of faith.

Headline:
"For by grace you have been saved through faith. And this is not your own doing; it is the gift of God, not a result of works, so that no one may boast." (Ephesians 2:8-9).

Reference:
"For we are God's workmanship, created in Christ Jesus to do good works, which God prepared in advance as our way of life." (Ephesians 2:10).

Headline:
"I give them eternal life, so that they will never perish. No one can snatch them out of My hand." (John 10:28).

Terms and Conditions:
"My sheep listen to My voice, I know them, and they follow Me." (John 10:27).

"To listen" and *"to follow"* here specifically indicate habitual actions.

Indeed, the sheep that stay faithful and obedient to the shepherd will never get lost!

Headline:
"I am sure that nothing can separate us from God's love—not life or death, not angels or spirits, not the present or the future, and not powers above or powers below.

Nothing in all creation can separate us from God's love for us in Christ Jesus our Lord!" (Romans 8:38-39).

Reference:
"So now there is no condemnation for those who belong to Christ Jesus who do not walk in the flesh, but in the Spirit." (Romans 8:1).

Indeed, nothing can separate us from God's love as long as we do not walk in the flesh, but in the Spirit.

Headline:
"If you confess that Jesus is Lord and
believe that God raised Him from death,
you will be saved." (Romans 10:9).

Terms and Conditions:
"Not everyone who calls me their Lord will get
into the kingdom of heaven. Only the ones
who obey my Father in heaven will get in."
(Matthew 7:21).

It is a fact that there are 31,102 verses
in the Bible. Some are *"headlines"* and the rest
are *"details"* (*"contexts"* and *"limitations"* etc).

You should have read the headlines
without ignoring their contexts with their terms
and conditions.

It's because everything in the Bible is true
and is contradiction free.

"..... teach them to do 'everything'
I have told you ....." (Matthew 28:20a).

No *"cherry-picking"* on God's Word!

CHAPTER 7
GRACE, FAITH, AND REWARD

Faith, Hope, and Love are BFF.

The three had just graduated from high school, but have no money for college.

One day, each of them receives a college grant offer, which is a need-based award of free money that doesn't require any repayment.

All they need to do is just accept the offers by signing the enclosed forms.

Faith is not interested and decides not to go to college but to work instead.

Hope and Love accept the offer. So, both of them sign up in good faith (no pun intended).

Once the two of them are in college, Hope's and Love's beliefs simply go their separate ways!

Hope believes that since she is already in college, her degree is automatically secured.

So, this award beneficiary is never serious with her student responsibility in college.

CHAPTER 7 GRACE, FAITH, AND REWARD

Love, on the other hand, believes that while college grant is a gift, a college degree is not.

So, she is committed to studying her best in order to earn her degree on graduation day.

The grace behind federal and state government grants is indeed universal.

College grants, however, are limited to those who, in good faith, accept the terms and conditions that come with the offer.

On the other hand, college degrees in fact are rewards, not freebies nor throw-ins!

The definition of a reward is:

"Something given in recognition of one's service, effort, or achievement."

So, reward is never granted but earned!

While college degrees are the goals that federal and state government have in view, they are in fact the students' responsibility.

As much as in this concept, there are aspects of grace, faith, and reward in salvation:

By grace, God had His begotten Son offer an atonement, not eternal life.

It is by grace that God has qualified you to participate. (Colossians 1:12)

By faith, those who believe in Him receive redemption from the slave market of sin.

"Now you have been set free from sin, and you are God's slaves. This will make you holy and will lead you to eternal life." (Romans 6:22).

So, having been redeemed as the slave to sin to become God's slave, you are now living under His laws and in His righteousness.

However, since eternal life is a reward, not a grace; only the faithful righteous and the righteous faithful will go into eternal life.

"But the righteous will go into eternal life." (Matthew 25:46b).

By grace, college grants, not college degrees; are being offered by the federal and state government.

By "faith", those who accept the offer by complying with relevant laws, policies, and regulations, are now qualified to receive college grants that pay for their education.

So, having received those grants, Hope and Love finally can afford to go to college.

However, since college degree is a reward, not a grace; only students who honor their education opportunity and work for it will earn their diplomas on graduation day.

Jesus Christ didn't come into this world to offer eternal life.

He never came to save people from the kingdom of earth to the kingdom of God.

Jesus Christ came into this world to make dead people live. He came so that those who are dead to God can come alive to God.

Christian faith is absolutely not child's play:

You: *"Jesus is Lord!"*
Jesus: *"Here's your 'reservation number' in kingdom of God."*

As a matter of fact, Christian faith is:

#1. A fight: *"Fight a good fight for the faith and claim eternal life."* (1 Timothy 6:12)

#2. A race: *"We must run the race that lies ahead of us and never give up."* (Hebrews 12:1b).

#3. A test: *"The purpose of these troubles is to test your faith as fire tests how genuine gold is."* (1 Peter 1:7a).

"Everyone who wins the victory will sit with Me on My throne, just as I won the victory and sat with My Father on his throne." (Revelation 3:21).

CHAPTER 8
DENY YOURSELF AND TAKE UP YOUR CROSS

"One of them, an expert in the law, tested Jesus with a question:

'Teacher, which commandment is the greatest in the Law?'

Jesus answered:

'Love the Lord your God with all your heart, soul, and mind'. This is the first and greatest commandment."
(Matthew 22:35-38).

How do you love the Lord your God with all your heart, soul, and mind?

#1. *"You must say no to the things you want, pick up your cross every day, and follow Him."*
(Luke 9:23)

#2. *"You must not have any other god but Me."*
(Exodus 20:3).

The word *"Lord"* is a translation from the word *"kurios"* in the original language of the New Testament, which means *"owner"*.

Kurios is an indicator of *"doulos"* (without any complexity, simply means *"slave"*).

Until somebody owns doulos (slave) as his *"property"*, he can't be called kurios (Lord), and vice versa.

For some reason, the vast majority of Bible versions in English translate the word *"doulos"* to the word *"servant"*.

As a matter of fact, slaves and servants are essentially different:

Slaves are purchased and owned as exclusive properties by their masters.

Slaves have no freedom and have no rights. They must obey whatever their masters tell them to do whenever and they work solely for their owners without pay.

Servants are laborers for hire. They are just rentals for a limited period of time. Servants have freedom and rights to work for whoever and whenever they like.

However, there is one advantage slaves have that servants don't:

Slaves are actual properties that must be taken good care of by their owners!

While Christians must call themselves slaves and Christ their sole owner, in fact, their Master calls them otherwise:

"I no longer call you slaves, because the slave does not understand what his master is doing. But I have called you friends, because I have revealed to you everything I heard from My Father." (John 15:15).

Denying yourselves means voluntarily stripping your rights and freedom for Christ.

Confessing Jesus as your Lord (Kurios) is explicitly proclaiming yourself as His slave (doulos):

"From Paul, a slave of Christ Jesus, called to be an apostle." (Romans 1:1).

CHAPTER 8 DENY YOURSELF AND TAKE UP YOUR CROSS

"From James, a slave of God and of the Lord Jesus Christ: Greetings to all God's people." (James 1:1).

"Epaphras, who is one of you, a slave of Christ Jesus, greets you." (Colossians 4:12).

"As the Lord's slave, you must not quarrel. You must be kind toward all, a good and patient teacher." (2 Timothy 2:24).

"From Simon Peter, a slave and apostle of Jesus Christ, to those who have been granted a faith just as precious as ours ......" (2 Peter 1:1a).

"From Jude, a slave of Jesus Christ and brother of James, to those who are called ....." (Jude 1:1).

"I am not trying to please people. I want to please God. Do you think I am trying to please people? If I were doing that, I would not be a slave of Christ." (Galatians 1:10).

"Remember what I told you: 'A slave is not greater than his master.' If they persecuted Me, they will also persecute you." (John 15:20a).

"You will be arrested, punished, and even killed. Because of Me, you will be hated by people of all nations." (Matthew 24:9).

"They strengthened the disciples in these cities and encouraged the disciples to continue in the faith. Paul and Barnabas told them, 'We must suffer a lot to enter the kingdom of God.'" (Acts 14:22).

"God called you to endure suffering because Christ suffered for you. He left you an example so that you could follow in His footsteps." (1 Peter 2:21).

It is plain and simple that Christians are called to endure a lot of suffering, which symbolizes the cross, in order to enter the kingdom of God.

It is completely true and can't be interpreted nor described as anything else.

Today, Christians belong to the largest religious group in not only America but the world.

Are they and their teachers and preachers suffering just like Christ who had suffered?

As a matter of fact, the vast majority of modern-day Christian life is a far cry from the way it is preached in the Bible!

Nowadays, Christians are indifferent, comfortable, cheerful, gluttonous, and enjoying their *"best life now"*.

They hang out and love to eat at church, friend, family gatherings, and whatnot!

"Fundamental Christians, particularly their pastors, are by far, prove to be the heaviest of all religious groups led by the Baptists with a 30% obesity rate compared with Jews at 1%, Buddhists and Hindus at 0.7% …. America is becoming a nation of gluttony and obesity, and churches are a feeding ground for this problem." (Ken Ferraro, the lead researcher on a Purdue study in 2006).

Studies confirm that more than 75% of American preachers are overweight— many of them to the point of obesity!

Scientifically, obesity is not a result of genetic and medical conditions but rather because of poor diet and lifestyle choices.

Today, many American Christians are in fact suffering for their *"fat"* more than for their faith!

Taking up your cross, a symbol of your suffering in Christ's footsteps, means that you must treasure Christ above all else the world has to offer, whether it is public approval, honor, comfort, or even your own life.

"You cannot be My disciple, unless you love Me more than you love your father and mother, your wife and children, and your brothers and sisters. You cannot follow Me unless you love Me more than you love your own life." (Luke 14:26).

"None of you can be My disciples unless you give up everything you have." (Luke 14:33).

"However, the suffering that Christians endure now cannot compare with the glory that will be shown to them." (Romans 8:18).

In fact, the suffering will
draw God even closer:

"The LORD is near to the brokenhearted and saves the crushed in spirit." (Psalms 34:18).

"He heals the brokenhearted and binds up their wounds." (Psalms 147:3).

*"For the High and Exalted One who lives forever, whose name is Holy says this:
'I live in a high and holy place,
and with the oppressed and lowly of spirit,
to revive the spirit of the lowly and
revive the heart of the oppressed.'"*
(Isaiah 57:15).

Christian faith is nothing short of voluntarily giving up everything you want in this kingdom of earth and getting your rewards in the kingdom of heaven.

You can never have both!

"The kingdom of heaven is like treasure, buried in a field, that a man found and reburied. Then in his joy he goes and sells everything he has and buys that field." (Matthew 13:44).

"And what do you benefit if you gain the whole world but lose your own soul? Is anything worth more than your soul?" (Matthew 16:26).

Every Christian on earth must *"think about the things of heaven, not the things of earth."* (Colossians 3:2).

CHAPTER 9
YOU MUST NOT HAVE ANY OTHER GOD BUT ME

When the Son of Man comes again,
the situation will be like the time of Noah
and Lot.

People were eating, drinking, buying and selling,
planting and building, and getting married.

They will be ungrateful, godless, heartless,
and hateful.

They will appear to have a godly life,
but they refuse to be transformed.

In the last days, people will love nobody
but themselves and money!

*"As Jesus was walking down a road,
a man ran up to him. He knelt down, and asked,*

*'Good teacher, what can I do to have eternal
life?'*

Jesus replied,

*'Why do you call me good?
Only God is good. You know the command-*

ments. 'Do not murder. Be faithful in marriage. Do not steal. Do not tell lies about others. Do not cheat. Respect your father and mother."

The man answered,

'Teacher, I have obeyed all these commandments since I was a young man.'

Jesus looked closely at the man. He liked him and said,

'There's one thing you still need to do. Go sell everything you own. Give the money to the poor, and you will have riches in heaven. Then come with Me.'

When the man heard Jesus say this, he went away gloomy and sad because he was very rich.

Jesus said:

'How hard it is for the rich to enter the kingdom of God!

In fact, it's easier for a camel to go through the eye of a needle than for a rich person to get into the kingdom of God.'"
(Mark 10:17-23,25).

This very rich gentleman was, in fact, well-prepared when he came to ask Jesus.

At least, he was ready with two presumptions and one expectation:

#1. Jesus was a good teacher

#2. He was a good man (for obeying the commandments)

#3. He was already good enough to have eternal life

When Jesus said, "Only God is good", He warned the gentleman that:

#1. Nobody was good in God's sight

#2. Not to presume anything with his self-sufficiency

In fact, Jesus proved point #2
by pointing at his self-insufficiency:

"There's one thing you still need to do".

At the end of the day, the gentleman preferred his money to eternal life.

He would rather lose his life than lose his money.

Point #1 was proven that nobody is good under any presumption but God's judgement!

"The love of money causes all kinds of trouble."
(1 Timothy 6:10).

Indeed, it's not money but the love of money that is the root of all kinds of evil!

However, it is not the $1 but the $1,000 that makes people start to care.

It is not the $1,000 but the $1,000,000 that makes people fall in love so hard.

It is just impossible not to love money, especially when there's a lot of it!

When the camel gets bigger, it is even more impossible to go through the eye of a needle!

Indeed, Christ never asks every Christian to sell everything and give their money to the poor.

He didn't ask Zacchaeus, the wealthy chief tax collector, to give even half of his possessions to the poor.

However, if Christ does ask you to go sell everything you own and give your money to the poor, what say you?

Anything that stands between a Christian and Christ is called idol!

"Jesus replied, 'You must love the LORD your God with all your heart, all your soul, and all your mind.'" (Matthew 22:37).

"You must not have any other god but Me." (Exodus 20:3).

CHAPTER 9 YOU MUST NOT HAVE ANY OTHER GOD BUT ME

"Dear children, keep away from anything that might take God's place in your hearts." (1 John 5:21).

Money, throne, self-image, ambition, business, career, lifestyle, gadgets, family, ideology, religion, institution, church, ministry.

It also includes everything in the world that your heart desires:

A craving for physical pleasure.
A craving for everything seen.
Pride in achievements and possessions.

"For from within the hearts of men come greed, arrogance, ……" (Mark 7:21-22).

Idols are living and hiding deep down in the bottom of the hearts.

That's where the slick mammon is ruling and turning many rich Christians, career teachers, and career preachers into quiet idolaters.

Pragmatically, rhetorically, or heretically!

"Don't you know if you love the world, you are God's enemies? And if you decide to be a friend of the world, you make yourself an enemy of God." (James 4:4).

"Don't love the world or anything that belongs to the world. If you love the world, you cannot love the Father.

"Our foolish pride comes from this world, and so do our selfish desires and our desire to have everything we see.

None of this comes from the Father. The world and the desires it causes are disappearing. But those who do the will of God live forever." (1 John 2:15-17).

"No idolaters will inherit the kingdom of God." (1 Corinthians 6:9, Revelation 22:15).

CHAPTER 10
FIRST LOVE

*The second greatest commandment
is like this one. And it is, 'Love others as much
as you love yourself'."* (Matthew 22:39).

How do you love others as much as
you love yourself?

You may have Christian faith
that can move mountains.
You may have supernatural gifts.
You may have the most successful
ministry in all nations.
And, you are ready to die for your faith.

However,
if you don't love others,
none of these things will help you.
(1 Corinthians 13:3).

It's because you have broken
the first and greatest commandment!

You can love others without loving the Lord
your God.

However, you can't never love the Lord
your God without loving others.

*For in the last days, "because sin is rampant
everywhere, most people's love will grow cold."
(Matthew 24:12).*

So will the love of most Christians!

*"I know your works, your labor,
and your patience. You have endured and gone
through hard times because of Me,
yet you have not given up.*

*But I have this against you:
You have abandoned your first love.
Therefore, keep in mind how far you have fallen.
Repent and perform the deeds you did at first.*

*But if you do not repent, I will come to you and
remove your lampstand from its place."
(Revelation 2:2a,3,4,5a).*

On judgement day, it is guaranteed that
you can't dodge the Son of Man
telling you:

"When I was hungry, you gave me something to eat, and when I was thirsty, you gave me something to drink. When I was a stranger, you welcomed me, and when I was naked, you gave me clothes to wear. When I was sick, you took care of me, and when I was in jail, you visited me.

Whenever you did it for any of my people, no matter how unimportant they seemed, you did it for me.

My father has blessed you! Come and receive the kingdom that was prepared for you before the world was created."
(Matthew 25:35,36,40,34)

or

"I was hungry, but you did not give me anything to eat, and I was thirsty, but you did not give me anything to drink. I was a stranger, but you did not welcome me, and I was naked, but you did not give me any clothes to wear. I was sick and in jail, but you did not take care of me.

*Whenever you failed to help any of my people,
no matter how unimportant they seemed,
you failed to do it for me.*

*Get away from me! You are under God's curse.
Go into the everlasting fire prepared
for the devil and his angels!"*
(Matthew 25:42,43,41).

As of now, which group do you belong to?

Your love for others proves your love for God.
Your love for God is the proof of your faith.
No love, no faith. No faith, no eternal life!

*"Children, you show love for others
by truly helping them, and not merely
by preaching about it."* (1 John 3:18).

Learn to love others like Mother Theresa!
She had chosen the right thing and
it would never be taken away from her.

When was the last time
you helped your brothers and sisters,
no matter how unimportant they seemed?

Love dies of cold, not of darkness!

"YOU MUST LOVE THE LORD YOUR GOD

WITH ALL YOUR HEART,

WITH ALL YOUR SOUL,

WITH ALL YOUR STRENGTH,

AND WITH ALL YOUR MIND.

AND YOU MUST LOVE YOUR NEIGHBOR

AS YOURSELF.

DO THIS,

AND YOU WILL LIVE."

(Matthew 10:27-28).

CONTEMPLATION

It is a fact that Christianity is the most embraced belief system like no other.

Ironically, however, the majority of those who identify as *"Christians"* are not Christians!

Scriptures have confirmed that only a few of them will ultimately be allowed into the kingdom of God. (Luke 13:23-24).

What gives?!

Aren't Christians saved not by works but by God's grace through faith alone in Jesus?

Did Christ not already die for my sins so nothing else matters?

Isn't it not what I do but what Christ has done to save me?

And the bottom line, is it not once saved always saved?

What did I miss?!

This mindset is thanks to the tradition of over-simplification of the salvation doctrine in child evangelism!

How would anyone practice faith they do not really understand?

How would they survive if they don't practice what they hear?

As a matter of fact, most Christians' biblical conception of the faith is only at the mercy of whoever evangelized or converted them!

Misinterpretation on salvation had turned into a misconception.

Misconception carved itself in stone and became a myth:

"A widely held but false idea or belief passed down through the generations."

The salvation myth has been evolving over generations and every generation has its own share of the myth.

Chain indoctrination in salvation pioneered by 4-14 evangelism has proven to make more heretic Christians than the biblical ones!

Salvation is not identical to eternal life.

The term "saved" or "having saved" is in fact unlike having *"a punched ticket to heaven or eternal life or kingdom of God"* whatsoever.

However, it refers to deliverance from sin or as known as redemption!

Jesus never came to offer eternal life but atonement.

Jesus never traded eternal life for Sinner's Prayers.

In fact, salvation is God's project initiated by His mercy and grace.

Salvation project is a lifelong pilgrimage for every Christian!

CONTEMPLATION

The project starts with God the Father giving His only begotten Son.

God the Son was sent into world to offer an atonement for the sins of the world.

Those who accept the offer will be saved from sin, delivered, born again, or redeemed.

The redeemed are no longer slaves to sin but God. In Christ they become new creations and no longer sin.

"Whoever is a believer in Christ is a new creation. The old way of living has disappeared. A new way of living has come into existence." (2 Corinthians 5:17).

"..... and to be renewed in the spirit of your mind and to put on the new self, created to be like God in true righteousness and holiness." (Ephesians 4:23-24).

"Each of you is now a new person. You are becoming more and more like your

Creator, and you will understand him better."
(Colossians 3:10).

"Those who live in Christ don't go on sinning. Those who go on sinning haven't seen or known Christ." (1 John 3:6).

"Those who have been born from God do not continue to sin, for God's very nature is in them; and because God is their Father, they cannot continue to sin." (1 John 3:9).

After Jesus returned to the Father, God the Holy Spirit came to help the redeemed continue to live in righteousness.

With the leadership and guidance of the Spirit of the Truth, every Christian must keep working to complete their own salvation with fear and trembling (Philippians 2:12b).

"Continue your fight for the Christian faith that was once and for all God has given to His people." (Jude 1:3).

If there's no grace, there's no atonement.
If there's no atonement, there's no faith.
If there's no faith, there's no redemption.
If there's no redemption,
there's no righteousness.
If there's no righteousness,
nobody can enter the kingdom of God.

You can never skip *"righteousness"* by going from *"faith"* all the way to *"eternal life"*!

Friedrich Nietzsche:
"I might believe in the Redeemer if His followers looked more redeemed."

People who claim themselves Christians or to have been "saved", but in fact still continue to sin, they are still slaves to sin.

They are not yet redeemed!

Unless you're redeemed,
you can't be righteous.

Unless you're righteous, you can't worship God in His kingdom of heaven.

Without righteousness, their Christian faith proves no more and no less than Christian myth!

At the end of the day,
the Lord knows those who belong to Him. Those who turn away from unrighteousness. (2 Timothy 2:19a).

At the end of the day,
the Lord also knows those who don't belong to Him. Those who don't turn away from unrighteousness.

"But He will say, 'I don't know you or where you're from. Get away from Me, all you workers of unrighteousness!'" (Luke 13:26-27).

By God's grace, Christ came to offer an atonement for the sins of the world.

By faith, people are redeemed from the slave market of sin.

By righteousness, the faithful will receive eternal life as a reward.

CONTEMPLATION

"But the righteous will go into eternal life."
(Matthew 25:46b).

It was atonement that made you qualified to participate in the race of faith to win the crown of life! (Colossians 1:12).

The reward of eternal life is guaranteed by God, but the recipients are not!

"So, run your best in the race of faith, and win eternal life for yourself; for it was to this life that God called you when you firmly professed your faith before many witnesses."
(1 Timothy 6:12).

Unless you love others as much as you love yourself, you can't love the Lord your God with all your heart, soul, and mind.

Unless you obey the greatest commandment, you can't be righteous. Unless you are righteous, you will not go to eternal life.

If your Christian life seems to be indifferent to others, you must be living with a myth, not faith!

"God's truth stands firm like a foundation stone with this inscription:

'The Lord knows those who belong to Him.

So, those who say that they belong to the Lord must turn away from unrighteousness!'"
(2 Timothy 3:19).

www.ingramcontent.com/pod-product-compliance
Lightning Source LLC
Chambersburg PA
CBHW021958290426
44108CB00012B/1121